From:

Date:

Message:

WORDS OF HOPE™

THE LORD IS MY SHEPHERD

christian art gifts®

The Lord Is My Shepherd

© 2016 Christian Art Gifts, RSA
　　　Christian Art Gifts Inc., IL, USA

First edition 2016

Designed by Christian Art Gifts

Images used under license from Shutterstock.com

Printed in China

ISBN 978-1-4321-1618-7

16 17 18 19 20 21 22 23 24 25 – 10 9 8 7 6 5 4 3 2 1

THE LORD IS MY SHEPHERD

The LORD is my shepherd;
I shall not want.
He makes me to lie down in green pastures;
He leads me beside the still waters.
He restores my soul;
He leads me in the paths of righteousness
for His name's sake.
Yea, though I walk through the
valley of the shadow of death,
I will fear no evil;
for You are with me;
Your rod and Your staff, they comfort me.
You prepare a table before me
in the presence of my enemies;
You anoint my head with oil;
my cup runs over.
Surely goodness and mercy shall follow me
all the days of my life;
and I will dwell in the house
of the LORD forever.

Psalm 23

Contents

The LORD is my Shepherd; I shall not want.

He Is Our Shepherd 10

We Are His Sheep 15

The Shepherd Provides 20

He makes me to lie down in green pastures;
He leads me beside the still waters.

The Shepherd Cares 26

In Him We Find Rest 31

He Gives Us Peace 36

We Need Not Worry 41

He restores my soul; He leads me in the paths of
righteousness for His name's sake.

He Restores Our Souls 47

He Guides Us 52

His Is the Path of Righteousness 57

The Name of the Lord Is Powerful 62

Yea, though I walk through the valley of the shadow of death, I will fear no evil; for You are with me; Your rod and Your staff, they comfort me.

He Is Our Help in Times of Trial 68

With Him by Our Side We Need Not Fear 73

He Is Always with Us 78

He Disciplines Those He Loves 83

In the Shepherd We Find Comfort 88

You prepare a table before me in the presence of my enemies; You anoint my head with oil; my cup runs over.

He Gives Us Victory over Our Enemies......................94

He Chose Us for Himself 99

He Blesses Every Day of Our Lives............................ 104

Surely goodness and mercy shall follow me all the days of my life; and I will dwell in the house of the LORD forever.

God Is Good.. 110

God Is Merciful 115

A Place in the House of the Lord................................ 120

Eternal Life with the Shepherd 125

The LORD
is my *Shepherd;*
I shall not want.

PSALM 23:1

 # HE IS OUR SHEPHERD

"I am the good shepherd. The good shepherd gives His life for the sheep."

John 10:11 NKJV

"I am the good shepherd. I know My own and My own know Me, just as the Father knows Me and I know the Father; and I lay down My life for the sheep."

John 10:14-15 ESV

He will feed His flock like a shepherd. He will carry the lambs in His arms, holding them close to His heart.

Isaiah 40:11 NLT

HE IS OUR SHEPHERD

"I Myself will tend My sheep and have them lie down, declares the Sovereign LORD. I will search for the lost and bring back the strays. I will bind up the injured and strengthen the weak. I will shepherd the flock with justice."

Ezekiel 34:15-16 NIV

He led His own people like a flock of sheep, guiding them safely through the wilderness.

Psalm 78:52 NLT

May the God of peace who brought up our Lord Jesus from the dead, that great Shepherd of the sheep, through the blood of the everlasting covenant, make you complete in every good work to do His will, working in you what is well pleasing in His sight, through Jesus Christ, to whom be glory forever and ever.

Hebrews 13:20-21 NKJV

HE IS OUR SHEPHERD

Save Your people, and bless Your inheritance; shepherd them also, and bear them up forever.

Psalm 28:9 NKJV

He will stand and shepherd His flock in the strength of the LORD, in the majesty of the name of the LORD His God. And they will live securely, for then His greatness will reach to the ends of the earth.

Micah 5:4 NIV

Give ear, O Shepherd of Israel, You who lead Joseph like a flock; You who dwell between the cherubim, shine forth!

Psalm 80:1 NKJV

For the Lamb at the center of the throne will be their shepherd; "He will lead them to springs of living water. And God will wipe away every tear from their eyes."

Revelation 7:17 NIV

Shepherd Your people with Your staff, the flock of Your heritage, who dwell solitarily in a woodland, in the midst of Carmel.

Micah 7:14 NKJV

"'And you, O Bethlehem, in the land of Judah, are by no means least among the rulers of Judah; for from you shall come a Ruler who will shepherd My people Israel.'"

Matthew 2:6 ESV

HE IS OUR SHEPHERD

Jesus said again, "Very truly I tell you, I am the gate for the sheep. All who have come before Me are thieves and robbers, but the sheep have not listened to them. I am the gate; whoever enters through Me will be saved. They will come in and go out, and find pasture. The thief comes only to steal and kill and destroy; I have come that they may have life, and have it to the full."

John 10:7-10 NIV

"When the Son of Man comes in His glory, and all the angels with Him, then He will sit on His glorious throne. Before Him will be gathered all the nations, and He will separate people one from another as a shepherd separates the sheep from the goats."

Matthew 25:31-32 ESV

WE ARE HIS SHEEP

Know that the LORD, He is God! It is He who made us, and we are His; we are His people, and the sheep of His pasture. Enter His gates with thanksgiving, and His courts with praise! Give thanks to Him; bless His name!

Psalm 100:3-4 ESV

"Do not be afraid, little flock, for your Father has been pleased to give you the kingdom."

Luke 12:32 NIV

We Your people, the sheep of Your pasture, will give thanks to You forever; from generation to generation we will recount Your praise.

Psalm 79:13 ESV

# WE ARE HIS SHEEP

"You are My flock, the flock of My pasture; you are men, and I am your God," says the Lord GOD.

Ezekiel 34:31 NKJV

Oh come, let us worship and bow down; let us kneel before the LORD, our Maker! For He is our God, and we are the people of His pasture, and the sheep of His hand.

Psalm 95:6-7 ESV

All of us, like sheep, have strayed away. We have left God's paths to follow our own. Yet the LORD laid on Him the sins of us all.

Isaiah 53:6 NLT

"Therefore this is what the Sovereign LORD says to them: See, I Myself will judge between the fat sheep and the lean sheep. Because you shove with flank and shoulder, butting all the weak sheep with your horns until you have driven them away, I will save My flock, and they will no longer be plundered."

Ezekiel 34:20-22 NIV

On that day the LORD their God will rescue His people, just as a shepherd rescues his sheep. They will sparkle in His land like jewels in a crown.

Zechariah 9:16 NLT

"My sheep listen to My voice; I know them, and they follow Me."

John 10:27 NIV

WE ARE HIS SHEEP

When He went ashore He saw a great crowd, and He had compassion on them, because they were like sheep without a shepherd. And He began to teach them many things.

Mark 6:34 ESV

Once you were like sheep who wandered away. But now you have turned to your Shepherd, the Guardian of your souls.

1 Peter 2:25 NLT

For thus says the Lord GOD: "Indeed I Myself will search for My sheep and seek them out. As a shepherd seeks out his flock on the day he is among his scattered sheep, so will I seek out My sheep and deliver them from all the places where they were scattered on a cloudy and dark day."

Ezekiel 34:11-12 NKJV

WE ARE HIS SHEEP

"The sheep hear His voice, and He calls His own sheep by name and leads them out. When He has brought out all His own, He goes before them, and the sheep follow Him, for they know His voice."

John 10:3-4 ESV

"What do you think? If a man owns a hundred sheep, and one of them wanders away, will he not leave the ninety-nine on the hills and go to look for the one that wandered off? And if he finds it, truly I tell you, he is happier about that one sheep than about the ninety-nine that did not wander off. In the same way your Father in heaven is not willing that any of these little ones should perish."

Matthew 18:12-14 NIV

"Your Father knows what you need before you ask Him."

Matthew 6:8 NIV

He provides food for those who fear Him;
He remembers His covenant forever.

Psalm 111:5 ESV

God shall supply all your need according to His riches in glory by Christ Jesus.

Philippians 4:19 NKJV

"Seek the Kingdom of God above all else, and live righteously, and He will give you everything you need."

Matthew 6:33 NLT

"Give, and it will be given to you. A good measure, pressed down, shaken together and running over, will be poured into your lap. For with the measure you use, it will be measured to you."

Luke 6:38 NIV

"Therefore do not be anxious, saying, 'What shall we eat?' or 'What shall we drink?' or 'What shall we wear?' For the Gentiles seek after all these things, and your heavenly Father knows that you need them all."

Matthew 6:31-32 ESV

"Consider the ravens, for they neither sow nor reap, which have neither storehouse nor barn; and God feeds them. Of how much more value are you than the birds?"

Luke 12:24 NKJV

"I will open the windows of heaven for you.
I will pour out a blessing so great you won't
have enough room to take it in. Try it! Put Me
to the test!"

Malachi 3:10 NLT

Fear the LORD, you His holy people, for those
who fear Him lack nothing. The lions may grow
weak and hungry, but those who seek the LORD
lack no good thing.

Psalm 34:9-10 NIV

The LORD is my shepherd; I have all that I need.

Psalm 23:1 NLT

THE SHEPHERD PROVIDES

He will give the rain for your land in its season, the early rain and the later rain, that you may gather in your grain and your wine and your oil. And He will give grass in your fields for your livestock, and you shall eat and be full.

Deuteronomy 11:14-15 ESV

"Every moving thing that lives shall be food for you. I have given you all things, even as the green herbs."

Genesis 9:3 NKJV

You care for the land and water it; You enrich it abundantly. The streams of God are filled with water to provide the people with grain, for so You have ordained it.

Psalm 65:9 NIV

# THE SHEPHERD PROVIDES

"Seek the Kingdom of God above all else, and He will give you everything you need."

Luke 12:31 NLT

He who supplies seed to the sower and bread for food will also supply and increase your store of seed and will enlarge the harvest of your righteousness. You will be enriched in every way so that you can be generous on every occasion, and through us your generosity will result in thanksgiving to God.

2 Corinthians 9:10-11 NIV

He makes me
to lie down in
green pastures;
He leads me beside
the still waters.

PSALM 23:2

THE SHEPHERD CARES

Cast your cares on the LORD and He will sustain you; He will never let the righteous be shaken.

Psalm 55:22 NIV

My help comes from the LORD, who made heaven and earth. He will not let your foot be moved; He who keeps you will not slumber.

Psalm 121:2-3 ESV

What is man that You are mindful of him, and the son of man that You visit him? For You have made him a little lower than the angels, and You have crowned him with glory and honor.

Psalm 8:4-5 NKJV

Cast all your anxiety on Him because He cares for you.

1 Peter 5:7 NIV

The LORD keeps you from all harm and watches over your life. The LORD keeps watch over you as you come and go, both now and forever.

Psalm 121:7-8 NLT

The LORD has been mindful of us; He will bless us; He will bless the house of Israel; He will bless the house of Aaron. He will bless those who fear the LORD, both small and great.

Psalm 115:12-13 NKJV

THE SHEPHERD CARES

I will be glad and rejoice in Your unfailing love, for You have seen my troubles, and You care about the anguish of my soul.

Psalm 31:7 NLT

"I will be your God throughout your lifetime – until your hair is white with age. I made you and I will care for you. I will carry you along and save you."

Isaiah 46:4 NLT

When I thought, "My foot slips," Your steadfast love, O LORD, held me up. When the cares of my heart are many, Your consolations cheer my soul.

Psalm 94:18-19 ESV

Those who are righteous will be long remembered. They do not fear bad news; they confidently trust the LORD to care for them.

Psalm 112:6-7 NLT

"Are not two sparrows sold for a copper coin? And not one of them falls to the ground apart from your Father's will. The very hairs of your head are all numbered. Do not fear therefore; you are of more value than many sparrows."

Matthew 10:29-31 NKJV

You go before me and follow me. You place Your hand of blessing on my head. Such knowledge is too wonderful for me, too great for me to understand!

Psalm 139:5-6 NLT

THE SHEPHERD CARES

"Can a woman forget her nursing child, that she should have no compassion on the son of her womb? Even these may forget, yet I will not forget you."

Isaiah 49:15 ESV

"Look at the lilies of the field and how they grow. They don't work or make their clothing, yet Solomon in all his glory was not dressed as beautifully as they are. And if God cares so wonderfully for wildflowers that are here today and thrown into the fire tomorrow, He will certainly care for you."

Matthew 6:28-30 NLT

 # IN HIM WE FIND REST

In peace I will lie down and sleep, for You alone, O Lord, will keep me safe.

Psalm 4:8 NLT

The Lord replied, "My Presence will go with you, and I will give you rest."

Exodus 33:14 NIV

Jesus said, "Come to Me, all of you who are weary and carry heavy burdens, and I will give you rest. Take My yoke upon you. Let Me teach you, because I am humble and gentle at heart, and you will find rest for your souls. For My yoke is easy to bear, and the burden I give you is light."

Matthew 11:28-30 NLT

IN HIM WE FIND REST

He said to them, "Come away by yourselves to a desolate place and rest a while."

Mark 6:31 ESV

This is what the Sovereign LORD, the Holy One of Israel, says: "Only in returning to Me and resting in Me will you be saved. In quietness and confidence is your strength. But you would have none of it."

Isaiah 30:15 NLT

Rest in the LORD, and wait patiently for Him; do not fret because of him who prospers in his way, because of the man who brings wicked schemes to pass.

Psalm 37:7 NKJV

IN HIM WE FIND REST

Those who live in the shelter of the Most High will find rest in the shadow of the Almighty. This I declare about the LORD: He alone is my refuge, my place of safety; He is my God, and I trust Him.

Psalm 91:1-2 NLT

The fear of the LORD leads to life; then one rests content, untouched by trouble.

Proverbs 19:23 NIV

"I have told you all this so that you may have peace in Me. Here on earth you will have many trials and sorrows. But take heart, because I have overcome the world."

John 16:33 NLT

IN HIM WE FIND REST

My soul finds rest in God; my salvation comes
from Him.

Psalm 62:1 NIV

The righteous man perishes, and no one lays
it to heart; devout men are taken away, while
no one understands. For the righteous man
is taken away from calamity; he enters into
peace; they rest in their beds who walk in their
uprightness.

Isaiah 57:1-2 ESV

He makes me to lie down in green pastures;
He leads me beside the still waters.

Psalm 23:2 NKJV

Unless the LORD builds a house, the work of
the builders is wasted ... It is useless for you
to work so hard from early morning until late
at night, anxiously working for food to eat;
for God gives rest to His loved ones.

Psalm 127:1-2 NLT

"Six days you shall labor, but on the seventh
day you shall rest; even during the plowing
season and harvest you must rest."

Exodus 34:21 NIV

I lay down and slept; I woke again, for the LORD
sustained me.

Psalm 3:5 ESV

"I am leaving you with a gift – peace of mind and heart. And the peace I give is a gift the world cannot give. So don't be troubled or afraid."

John 14:27 NLT

The mind governed by the Spirit is life and peace.

Romans 8:6 NIV

The LORD sits enthroned over the flood; the LORD is enthroned as King forever. The LORD gives strength to His people; the LORD blesses His people with peace.

Psalm 29:10-11 NIV

HE GIVES US PEACE

Because of God's tender mercy, the morning light from heaven is about to break upon us, to give light to those who sit in darkness and in the shadow of death, to guide us to the path of peace.

Luke 1:78-79 NLT

Great peace have those who love Your law, and nothing can make them stumble. I wait for Your salvation, LORD, and I follow Your commands.

Psalm 119:165-166 NIV

Let the peace of Christ rule in your hearts.

Colossians 3:15 ESV

You will keep in perfect peace those whose minds are steadfast, because they trust in You.

Isaiah 26:3 NIV

Those who are peacemakers will plant seeds of peace and reap a harvest of righteousness.

James 3:18 NLT

"Glory to God in the highest heaven, and on earth peace to those on whom His favor rests."

Luke 2:14 NIV

God is not a God of confusion but of peace.

1 Corinthians 14:33 ESV

HE GIVES US PEACE

Submit to God and be at peace with Him;
in this way prosperity will come to you.

Job 22:21 NIV

The meek shall inherit the earth, and shall
delight themselves in the abundance of peace.

Psalm 37:11 NKJV

The God of peace be with you.

Romans 15:33 NIV

The work of righteousness will be peace,
and the effect of righteousness, quietness
and assurance forever.

Isaiah 32:17 NKJV

When a man's ways please the LORD, He makes
even his enemies to be at peace with him.

Proverbs 16:7 ESV

May the God of hope fill you with all joy and
peace as you trust in Him, so that you may
overflow with hope by the power of the Holy
Spirit.

Romans 15:13 NIV

May God give you more and more mercy, peace,
and love.

Jude 2 NLT

Commit everything you do to the LORD. Trust Him, and He will help you.

Psalm 37:5 NLT

Do not be anxious about anything, but in every situation, by prayer and petition, with thanksgiving, present your requests to God. And the peace of God, which transcends all understanding, will guard your hearts and your minds in Christ Jesus.

Philippians 4:6-7 NIV

Overwhelming victory is ours through Christ, who loved us.

Romans 8:37 NLT

WE NEED NOT WORRY

In You, O LORD, I put my trust; let me never be put to shame.

Psalm 71:1 NKJV

I keep my eyes always on the LORD. With Him at my right hand, I will not be shaken. Therefore my heart is glad and my tongue rejoices; my body also will rest secure, because You will not abandon me.

Psalm 16:8-10 NIV

Do not be afraid and do not panic before them. For the LORD your God will personally go ahead of you. He will neither fail you nor abandon you.

Deuteronomy 31:6 NLT

WE NEED NOT WORRY

In His hand is the life of every creature and the breath of all mankind.

Job 12:10 NIV

Do not be afraid or discouraged, for the LORD will personally go ahead of you. He will be with you; He will neither fail you nor abandon you.

Deuteronomy 31:8 NLT

"Therefore I tell you, do not be anxious about your life, what you will eat or what you will drink. Look at the birds of the air: they neither sow nor reap nor gather into barns, and yet your heavenly Father feeds them. Are you not of more value than they?"

Matthew 6:25-26 ESV

WE NEED NOT WORRY

Anxiety weighs down the heart, but a kind word cheers it up.

Proverbs 12:25 NIV

"Do not be anxious about how you should defend yourself or what you should say, for the Holy Spirit will teach you in that very hour what you ought to say."

Luke 12:11-12 ESV

You will keep in perfect peace all who trust in You, all whose thoughts are fixed on You! Trust in the Lord always, for the Lord God is the eternal Rock.

Isaiah 26:3-4 NLT

"Be still, and know that I am God. I will be exalted among the nations, I will be exalted in the earth!" The LORD of hosts is with us; the God of Jacob is our fortress.

Psalm 46:10-11 ESV

"Fear not, for I have redeemed you; I have called you by your name; you are Mine."

Isaiah 43:1 NKJV

"Therefore do not be anxious about tomorrow, for tomorrow will be anxious for itself. Sufficient for the day is its own trouble."

Matthew 6:34 ESV

He restores my soul;

He leads me in the

paths of *righteousness*

for His name's sake.

PSALM 23:3

The LORD sustains them on their sickbed and restores them from their bed of illness.

Psalm 41:3 NIV

In His kindness God called you to share in His eternal glory by means of Christ Jesus. So after you have suffered a little while, He will restore, support, and strengthen you, and He will place you on a firm foundation.

1 Peter 5:10 NLT

He restores my soul; He leads me in the paths of righteousness for His name's sake.

Psalm 23:3 NKJV

Therefore we do not lose heart. Though outwardly we are wasting away, yet inwardly we are being renewed day by day.

2 Corinthians 4:16 NIV

"Return to the stronghold, you prisoners of hope. Even today I declare that I will restore double to you."

Zechariah 9:12 NKJV

Though You have made me see troubles, many and bitter, You will restore my life again; from the depths of the earth You will again bring me up.

Psalm 71:20 NIV

Therefore, if anyone is in Christ, he is a new creation; old things have passed away; behold, all things have become new.

2 Corinthians 5:17 NKJV

Aim for restoration, comfort one another, agree with one another, live in peace; and the God of love and peace will be with you.

2 Corinthians 13:11 ESV

God will wipe away every tear from their eyes; there shall be no more death, nor sorrow, nor crying. There shall be no more pain, for the former things have passed away.

Revelation 21:4 NKJV

HE RESTORES OUR SOULS

Do not conform to the pattern of this world, but be transformed by the renewing of your mind. Then you will be able to test and approve what God's will is – His good, pleasing and perfect will.

Romans 12:2 NIV

I will exalt You, LORD, for You rescued me. You refused to let my enemies triumph over me. O LORD my God, I cried to You for help, and You restored my health.

Psalm 30:1-2 NLT

Restore to me the joy of Your salvation and grant me a willing spirit, to sustain me.

Psalm 51:12 NIV

HE RESTORES OUR SOULS

Those who wait on the LORD shall renew their strength; they shall mount up with wings like eagles, they shall run and not be weary, they shall walk and not faint.

Isaiah 40:31 NKJV

Repent of your sins and turn to God, so that your sins may be wiped away. Then times of refreshment will come from the presence of the Lord, and He will again send you Jesus, your appointed Messiah. For He must remain in heaven until the time for the final restoration of all things, as God promised long ago through His holy prophets.

Acts 3:19-21 NLT

"I will refresh the weary and satisfy the faint."

Jeremiah 31:25 NIV

HE GUIDES US

The LORD will guide you always; He will satisfy your needs in a sun-scorched land and will strengthen your frame. You will be like a well-watered garden, like a spring whose waters never fail.

Isaiah 58:11 NIV

Jesus said to him, "I am the way, the truth, and the life. No one comes to the Father except through Me."

John 14:6 NKJV

Show me Your ways, LORD, teach me Your paths. Guide me in Your truth and teach me, for You are God my Savior, and my hope is in You all day long.

Psalm 25:4-5 NIV

HE GUIDES US

Send out Your light and Your truth; let them guide me. Let them lead me to Your holy mountain, to the place where You live. There I will go to the altar of God, to God – the source of all my joy.

Psalm 43:3-4 NLT

"Call to Me, and I will answer you, and show you great and mighty things, which you do not know."

Jeremiah 33:3 NKJV

Your word is a lamp to guide my feet and a light for my path.

Psalm 119:105 NLT

Teach me to do Your will, for You are my God!
Let Your good Spirit lead me on level ground!
For Your name's sake, O LORD, preserve my
life! In Your righteousness bring my soul out
of trouble!

Psalm 143:10-11 ESV

May the Lord direct your hearts into God's love
and Christ's perseverance.

2 Thessalonians 3:5 NIV

The LORD directs the steps of the godly. He
delights in every detail of their lives. Though
they stumble, they will never fall, for the LORD
holds them by the hand.

Psalm 37:23-24 NLT

HE GUIDES US

Whether you turn to the right or to the left, your ears will hear a voice behind you, saying, "This is the way; walk in it."

Isaiah 30:21 NIV

Direct my steps by Your word, and let no iniquity have dominion over me.

Psalm 119:133 NKJV

All who are led by the Spirit of God are children of God.

Romans 8:14 NLT

God is our God for ever and ever; He will be our guide even to the end.

Psalm 48:14 NIV

HE GUIDES US

"I will go before you and make the crooked places straight; I will break in pieces the gates of bronze and cut the bars of iron."

Isaiah 45:2 NKJV

The LORD says, "I will guide you along the best pathway for your life. I will advise you and watch over you."

Psalm 32:8 NLT

May He give you the desire of your heart and make all your plans succeed.

Psalm 20:4 NIV

HIS IS THE PATH OF RIGHTEOUSNESS

Since we know that Christ is righteous, we also know that all who do what is right are God's children.

1 John 2:29 NLT

Righteous are You, O LORD, and upright are Your judgments. Your testimonies, which You have commanded, are righteous and very faithful.

Psalm 119:137-138 NKJV

In Your righteousness, rescue me and deliver me; turn Your ear to me and save me.

Psalm 71:2 NIV

HIS IS THE PATH OF RIGHTEOUSNESS

As for the Almighty, we cannot find Him; He is excellent in power, in judgment and abundant justice; He does not oppress.

Job 37:23 NKJV

He judges the world with righteousness;
He judges the peoples with uprightness.

Psalm 9:8 ESV

The LORD loves righteousness and justice;
the earth is full of His unfailing love.

Psalm 33:5 NIV

My tongue shall speak of Your righteousness
and of Your praise all the day long.

Psalm 35:28 NKJV

HIS IS THE PATH OF RIGHTEOUSNESS

Your righteousness is like the mighty mountains, Your justice like the ocean depths. You care for people and animals alike, O LORD.

Psalm 36:6 NLT

My mouth will tell of Your righteous deeds, of Your saving acts all day long – though I know not how to relate them all. I will come and proclaim Your mighty acts, Sovereign LORD; I will proclaim Your righteous deeds, Yours alone. Since my youth, God, You have taught me, and to this day I declare Your marvelous deeds.

Psalm 71:15-17 NIV

Your righteousness, O God, reaches the high heavens. You who have done great things, O God, who is like You?

Psalm 71:19 ESV

HIS IS THE PATH OF RIGHTEOUSNESS

The LORD gives righteousness and justice to all who are treated unfairly.

Psalm 103:6 NLT

Your righteousness is an everlasting righteousness, and Your law is truth.

Psalm 119:142 NKJV

Therefore, since we have been made right in God's sight by faith, we have peace with God because of what Jesus Christ our Lord has done for us. Because of our faith, Christ has brought us into this place of undeserved privilege where we now stand, and we confidently and joyfully look forward to sharing God's glory.

Romans 5:1-2 NLT

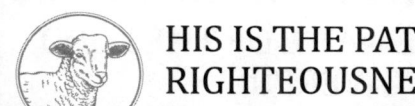

HIS IS THE PATH OF RIGHTEOUSNESS

No human being might boast in the presence of God. And because of Him you are in Christ Jesus, who became to us wisdom from God, righteousness and sanctification and redemption, so that, as it is written, "Let the one who boasts, boast in the Lord."

1 Corinthians 1:29-31 ESV

The LORD of Heaven's Armies will be exalted by His justice. The holiness of God will be displayed by His righteousness.

Isaiah 5:16 NLT

God made Him who had no sin to be sin for us, so that in Him we might become the righteousness of God.

2 Corinthians 5:21 NIV

Everyone who calls on the name of the LORD will be saved.

Romans 10:13 NLT

Sing to God, sing in praise of His name, extol Him who rides on the clouds; rejoice before Him – His name is the LORD.

Psalm 68:4 NIV

You were cleansed; you were made holy; you were made right with God by calling on the name of the Lord Jesus Christ and by the Spirit of our God.

1 Corinthians 6:11 NLT

THE NAME OF THE LORD IS POWERFUL

There is none like You, O LORD; You are great, and Your name is great in might.

Jeremiah 10:6 ESV

The name of the LORD is a fortified tower; the righteous run to it and are safe.

Proverbs 18:10 NIV

"My name is honored by people of other nations from morning till night. All around the world they offer sweet incense and pure offerings in honor of My name. For My name is great among the nations," says the LORD of Heaven's Armies.

Malachi 1:11 NLT

THE NAME OF THE LORD IS POWERFUL

"Whatever you ask in My name, this I will do, that the Father may be glorified in the Son. If you ask Me anything in My name, I will do it."

John 14:13-14 ESV

Praise the LORD. Praise the LORD, you His servants; praise the name of the LORD. Let the name of the LORD be praised, both now and forevermore. From the rising of the sun to the place where it sets, the name of the LORD is to be praised.

Psalm 113:1-3 NIV

"She will bear a Son, and you shall call His name Jesus, for He will save His people from their sins."

Matthew 1:21 ESV

"And these signs will follow those who believe: In My name they will cast out demons; they will speak with new tongues; they will take up serpents; and if they drink anything deadly, it will by no means hurt them; they will lay hands on the sick, and they will recover."

Mark 16:17-18 NKJV

Moses protested, "If I go to the people of Israel and tell them, 'The God of your ancestors has sent me to you,' they will ask me, 'What is His name?' Then what should I tell them?" God replied to Moses, "I AM WHO I AM. Say this to the people of Israel: I AM has sent me to you."

Exodus 3:13-14 NLT

THE NAME OF THE LORD IS POWERFUL

For unto us a Child is born, unto us a Son is given; and the government will be upon His shoulder. And His name will be called Wonderful, Counselor, Mighty God, Everlasting Father, Prince of Peace.

Isaiah 9:6 NKJV

God also has highly exalted Him and given Him the name which is above every name, that at the name of Jesus every knee should bow, of those in heaven, and of those on earth, and of those under the earth, and that every tongue should confess that Jesus Christ is Lord, to the glory of God the Father.

Philippians 2:9-11 NKJV

Yea, though I walk through the *valley* of the shadow of death, I will fear no evil; for You are with me; Your rod and Your staff, they *comfort me.*

PSALM 23:4

HE IS OUR HELP IN TIMES OF TRIAL

Blessed is the one who perseveres under trial because, having stood the test, that person will receive the crown of life.

James 1:12 NIV

We rejoice in our sufferings, knowing that suffering produces endurance, and endurance produces character, and character produces hope, and hope does not put us to shame, because God's love has been poured into our hearts through the Holy Spirit who has been given to us.

Romans 5:3-5 ESV

Since He Himself has gone through suffering and testing, He is able to help us when we are being tested.

Hebrews 2:18 NLT

HE IS OUR HELP IN TIMES OF TRIAL

Consider it pure joy, my brothers and sisters, whenever you face trials of many kinds, because you know that the testing of your faith develops perseverance. Let perseverance finish its work so that you may be mature and complete, not lacking anything.

James 1:2-4 NIV

I consider that the sufferings of this present time are not worth comparing with the glory that is to be revealed to us.

Romans 8:18 ESV

As the elect of God, holy and beloved, put on tender mercies, kindness, humility, meekness, longsuffering.

Colossians 3:12 NKJV

HE IS OUR HELP IN TIMES OF TRIAL

Beloved, do not think it strange concerning the fiery trial which is to try you, as though some strange thing happened to you; but rejoice to the extent that you partake of Christ's sufferings, that when His glory is revealed, you may also be glad with exceeding joy.

1 Peter 4:12-13 NKJV

God had planned something better for us.

Hebrews 11:40 NIV

The more we suffer for Christ, the more God will shower us with His comfort through Christ.

2 Corinthians 1:5 NLT

HE IS OUR HELP IN TIMES OF TRIAL

Those who suffer according to God's will should commit themselves to their faithful Creator and continue to do good.

1 Peter 4:19 NIV

"When you go through deep waters, I will be with you. When you go through rivers of difficulty, you will not drown. When you walk through the fire of oppression, you will not be burned up; the flames will not consume you."

Isaiah 43:2 NLT

If you suffer for doing good and you endure it, this is commendable before God.

1 Peter 2:20 NIV

HE IS OUR HELP IN TIMES OF TRIAL

I love the LORD because He hears my voice and my prayer for mercy. Because He bends down to listen, I will pray as long as I have breath!

Psalm 116:1-2 NLT

Be strong and do not give up, for your work will be rewarded.

2 Chronicles 15:7 NIV

Let us throw off everything that hinders and the sin that so easily entangles. And let us run with perseverance the race marked out for us.

Hebrews 12:1 NIV

WITH HIM BY OUR SIDE WE NEED NOT FEAR

He will cover you with His pinions, and under His wings you will find refuge; His faithfulness is a shield and buckler. You will not fear the terror of the night, nor the arrow that flies by day, nor the pestilence that stalks in darkness, nor the destruction that wastes at noonday.

Psalm 91:4-6 ESV

"So do not fear, for I am with you; do not be dismayed, for I am your God."

Isaiah 41:10 NIV

The LORD is my light and my salvation; whom shall I fear? The LORD is the strength of my life; of whom shall I be afraid?

Psalm 27:1 NKJV

WITH HIM BY OUR SIDE WE NEED NOT FEAR

Even though I walk through the valley of the shadow of death, I will fear no evil, for You are with me; Your rod and Your staff, they comfort me.

Psalm 23:4 ESV

Be strong, and do not fear, for your God is coming to destroy your enemies. He is coming to save you.

Isaiah 35:4 NLT

"I am the LORD your God who takes hold of your right hand and says to you, 'Do not fear; I will help you.'"

Isaiah 41:13 NIV

WITH HIM BY OUR SIDE
WE NEED NOT FEAR

When I am afraid, I will put my trust in You. I praise God for what He has promised. I trust in God, so why should I be afraid? What can mere mortals do to me?

Psalm 56:3-4 NLT

"Have I not commanded you? Be strong and courageous. Do not be frightened, and do not be dismayed, for the LORD your God is with you wherever you go."

Joshua 1:9 ESV

God is our refuge and strength, an ever-present help in trouble.

Psalm 46:1 NIV

WITH HIM BY OUR SIDE
WE NEED NOT FEAR

God has said, "I will never fail you. I will never abandon you." So we can say with confidence, "The LORD is my helper, so I will have no fear. What can mere people do to me?"

Hebrews 13:5-6 NLT

The fear of man brings a snare, but whoever trusts in the LORD shall be safe.

Proverbs 29:25 NKJV

God has not given us a spirit of fear and timidity, but of power, love, and self-discipline.

2 Timothy 1:7 NLT

WITH HIM BY OUR SIDE
WE NEED NOT FEAR

The angel of the LORD encamps all around those who fear Him, and delivers them.

Psalm 34:7 NKJV

I sought the LORD, and He answered me and delivered me from all my fears.

Psalm 34:4 ESV

There is no fear in love. But perfect love drives out fear, because fear has to do with punishment. The one who fears is not made perfect in love.

1 John 4:18 NIV

HE IS ALWAYS WITH US

"The kingdom of God is within you."

Luke 17:21 NKJV

Let us hold fast the confession of our hope without wavering, for He who promised is faithful.

Hebrews 10:23 ESV

"Where two or three are gathered together in My name, I am there in the midst of them."

Matthew 18:20 NKJV

Because of Christ and our faith in Him, we can now come boldly and confidently into God's presence.

Ephesians 3:12 NLT

HE IS ALWAYS WITH US

"Anyone who loves Me will obey My teaching. My Father will love them, and We will come to them and make Our home with them."

John 14:23 NIV

Surely Your goodness and unfailing love will pursue me all the days of my life, and I will live in the house of the LORD forever.

Psalm 23:6 NLT

The LORD your God is with you, the Mighty Warrior who saves. He will take great delight in you; in His love He will no longer rebuke you, but will rejoice over you with singing.

Zephaniah 3:17 NIV

There is one Lord, one faith, one baptism, one God and Father of all, who is over all, in all, and living through all.

Ephesians 4:5-6 NLT

The eyes of the LORD are in every place, keeping watch on the evil and the good.

Proverbs 15:3 NKJV

"If you look for Me wholeheartedly, you will find Me."

Jeremiah 29:13 NLT

God is with those who obey Him.

Psalm 14:5 NLT

"Where were you when I laid the foundations of the earth? Tell Me, if you have understanding. Who determined its measurements? Surely you know! Or who stretched the line upon it? To what were its foundations fastened? Or who laid its cornerstone, when the morning stars sang together, and all the sons of God shouted for joy?"

Job 38:4-7 NKJV

God watches how people live; He sees everything they do.

Job 34:21 NLT

He is before all things, and in Him all things hold together.

Colossians 1:17 ESV

Can you solve the mysteries of God? Can you
discover everything about the Almighty?
Such knowledge is higher than the heavens –
and who are you? It is deeper than the under-
world – what do you know? It is broader than
the earth and wider than the sea.

Job 11:7-9 NLT

For the word of God is alive and active. Sharper
than any double-edged sword, it penetrates
even to dividing soul and spirit, joints and
marrow; it judges the thoughts and attitudes
of the heart. Nothing in all creation is hidden
from God's sight. Everything is uncovered and
laid bare before the eyes of Him to whom we
must give account.

Hebrews 4:12-13 NIV

HE DISCIPLINES THOSE HE LOVES

Don't make light of the LORD's discipline, and don't give up when He corrects you. For the LORD disciplines those He loves, and He punishes each one He accepts as His child.

Hebrews 12:5-6 NLT

Do not despise the chastening of the LORD, nor detest His correction; for whom the LORD loves He corrects, just as a father the son in whom he delights.

Proverbs 3:11-12 NKJV

Our light and momentary troubles are achieving for us an eternal glory that far outweighs them all. So we fix our eyes not on what is seen, but on what is unseen, since what is seen is temporary, but what is unseen is eternal.

2 Corinthians 4:17-18 NIV

HE DISCIPLINES THOSE HE LOVES

"Those whom I love, I reprove and discipline, so be zealous and repent."

Revelation 3:19 ESV

Think about it: Just as a parent disciplines a child, the LORD your God disciplines you for your own good.

Deuteronomy 8:5 NLT

If you endure chastening, God deals with you as with sons; for what son is there whom a father does not chasten? But if you are without chastening, of which all have become partakers, then you are illegitimate and not sons.

Hebrews 12:7-8 NKJV

HE DISCIPLINES THOSE HE LOVES

This is what the LORD says – your Redeemer, the Holy One of Israel: "I am the LORD your God, who teaches you what is best for you, who directs you in the way you should go."

Isaiah 48:17 NIV

When we are judged by the Lord, we are disciplined so that we may not be condemned along with the world.

1 Corinthians 11:32 ESV

Behold, happy is the man whom God corrects; therefore do not despise the chastening of the Almighty.

Job 5:17 NKJV

HE DISCIPLINES THOSE HE LOVES

Joyful are those You discipline, LORD, those You teach with Your instructions. You give them relief from troubled times until a pit is dug to capture the wicked.

Psalm 94:12-13 NLT

For the moment all discipline seems painful rather than pleasant, but later it yields the peaceful fruit of righteousness to those who have been trained by it.

Hebrews 12:11 ESV

If you reject discipline, you only harm yourself; but if you listen to correction, you grow in understanding.

Proverbs 15:32 NIV

HE DISCIPLINES THOSE HE LOVES

Since we respected our earthly fathers who disciplined us, shouldn't we submit even more to the discipline of the Father of our spirits, and live forever? For our earthly fathers disciplined us for a few years, doing the best they knew how. But God's discipline is always good for us, so that we might share in His holiness.

Hebrews 12:9-10 NLT

Whoever loves discipline loves knowledge.

Proverbs 12:1 ESV

Whoever heeds discipline shows the way to life, but whoever ignores correction leads others astray.

Proverbs 10:17 NIV

IN THE SHEPHERD WE FIND COMFORT

"Do not be afraid, for I am with you; I will bless you."

Genesis 26:24 NIV

You give them relief from troubled times. The LORD will not reject His people; He will not abandon His special possession.

Psalm 94:13-14 NLT

He heals the brokenhearted and binds up their wounds.

Psalm 147:3 NIV

Let Your unfailing love comfort me, just as You promised me.

Psalm 119:76 NLT

IN THE SHEPHERD
WE FIND COMFORT

"Blessed are those who mourn, for they will be comforted."

Matthew 5:4 NIV

Praise be to the God and Father of our Lord Jesus Christ, the Father of compassion and the God of all comfort, who comforts us in all our troubles.

2 Corinthians 1:3-4 NIV

Give me a sign of Your goodness, that my enemies may see it and be put to shame, for You, LORD, have helped me and comforted me.

Psalm 86:17 NIV

IN THE SHEPHERD WE FIND COMFORT

Though I walk in the midst of trouble, You preserve my life; You stretch out Your hand against the wrath of my enemies, and Your right hand delivers me.

Psalm 138:7 ESV

As the deer longs for streams of water, so I long for You, O God. I thirst for God, the living God. When can I go and stand before Him?

Psalm 42:1-2 NLT

Shout for joy, you heavens; rejoice, you earth; burst into song, you mountains! For the Lord comforts His people and will have compassion on His afflicted ones.

Isaiah 49:13 NIV

IN THE SHEPHERD WE FIND COMFORT

The LORD upholds all who fall, and raises up all who are bowed down.

Psalm 145:14 NKJV

The LORD is close to the brokenhearted; He rescues those whose spirits are crushed.

Psalm 34:18 NLT

"Can a mother forget the baby at her breast and have no compassion on the child she has borne? Though she may forget, I will not forget you! See, I have engraved you on the palms of My hands; your walls are ever before Me."

Isaiah 49:15-16 NIV

Weeping may endure for a night, but joy comes in the morning.

Psalm 30:5 NKJV

"As a mother comforts her child, so will I comfort you."

Isaiah 66:13 NIV

"I, yes I, am the one who comforts you. So why are you afraid?"

Isaiah 51:12 NLT

This is my comfort in my affliction, that Your promise gives me life.

Psalm 119:50 ESV

You *prepare*
a table before me
in the presence
of my enemies;
You anoint
my head with oil;
my cup runs over.

PSALM 23:5

HE GIVES US VICTORY OVER OUR ENEMIES

Thanks be to God! He gives us the victory through our Lord Jesus Christ.

1 Corinthians 15:57 NIV

Thanks be to God who always leads us in triumph in Christ, and through us diffuses the fragrance of His knowledge in every place.

2 Corinthians 2:14 NKJV

Some nations boast of their chariots and horses, but we boast in the name of the LORD our God. Those nations will fall down and collapse, but we will rise up and stand firm.

Psalm 20:7-8 NLT

HE GIVES US VICTORY OVER OUR ENEMIES

Through God we will do valiantly, for it is He who shall tread down our enemies.

Psalm 60:12 NKJV

Songs of joy and victory are sung in the camp of the godly. The strong right arm of the LORD has done glorious things!

Psalm 118:15 NLT

The LORD your God is the one who goes with you to fight for you against your enemies to give you victory.

Deuteronomy 20:4 NIV

HE GIVES US VICTORY OVER OUR ENEMIES

We know that God causes everything to work together for the good of those who love God and are called according to His purpose for them.

Romans 8:28 NLT

It was not by their sword that they won the land, nor did their arm bring them victory; it was Your right hand, Your arm, and the light of Your face, for You loved them.

Psalm 44:3 NIV

The horse is made ready for the day of battle, but the victory belongs to the LORD.

Proverbs 21:31 ESV

HE GIVES US VICTORY OVER OUR ENEMIES

The LORD gives victory to His anointed. He answers him from His heavenly sanctuary with the victorious power of His right hand.

Psalm 20:6 NIV

The LORD shall go forth like a mighty man;
He shall stir up His zeal like a man of war. He shall cry out, yes, shout aloud; He shall prevail against His enemies.

Isaiah 42:13 NKJV

I put no trust in my bow, my sword does not bring me victory; but You give us victory over our enemies, You put our adversaries to shame.

Psalm 44:6-7 NIV

HE GIVES US VICTORY OVER OUR ENEMIES

He has delivered me from every trouble, and my eye has looked in triumph on my enemies.

Psalm 54:7 ESV

When the righteous triumph, there is great elation; but when the wicked rise to power, people go into hiding.

Proverbs 28:12 NIV

You are a chosen generation, a royal priest-hood, a holy nation, His own special people, that you may proclaim the praises of Him who called you out of darkness into His marvelous light.

1 Peter 2:9 NKJV

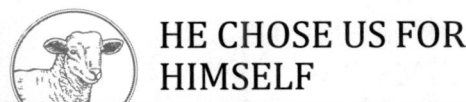
Victory comes from You, O LORD. May You bless Your people.

Psalm 3:8 NLT

We are His workmanship, created in Christ Jesus for good works, which God prepared beforehand that we should walk in them.

Ephesians 2:10 NKJV

For He chose us in Him before the creation of the world to be holy and blameless in His sight. In love He predestined us for adoption to sonship through Jesus Christ, in accordance with His pleasure and will – to the praise of His glorious grace, which He has freely given us in the One He loves.

Ephesians 1:4-6 NIV

HE CHOSE US FOR HIMSELF

In Him we were also chosen, having been predestined according to the plan of Him who works out everything in conformity with the purpose of His will, in order that we, who were the first to put our hope in Christ, might be for the praise of His glory.

Ephesians 1:11-12 NIV

God knew His people in advance, and He chose them to become like His Son, so that His Son would be the firstborn among many brothers and sisters. And having chosen them, He called them to come to Him. And having called them, He gave them right standing with Himself. And having given them right standing, He gave them His glory.

Romans 8:29-30 NLT

HE CHOSE US FOR HIMSELF

"You did not choose Me, but I chose you and appointed you that you should go and bear fruit and that your fruit should abide, so that whatever you ask the Father in My name, He may give it to you."

John 15:16 ESV

You are a holy people to the LORD your God; the LORD your God has chosen you to be a people for Himself, a special treasure above all the peoples on the face of the earth.

Deuteronomy 7:6 NKJV

You have been set apart as holy to the LORD your God, and He has chosen you from all the nations of the earth to be His own special treasure.

Deuteronomy 14:2 NLT

HE CHOSE US FOR HIMSELF

"Before I formed you in the womb I knew you, before you were born I set you apart; I appointed you as a prophet to the nations."

Jeremiah 1:5 NIV

He is Lord of lords and King of kings; and those who are with Him are called, chosen, and faithful.

Revelation 17:14 NKJV

To all who did receive Him, who believed in His name, He gave the right to become children of God, who were born, not of blood nor of the will of the flesh nor of the will of man, but of God.

John 1:12-13 ESV

HE CHOSE US FOR HIMSELF

Know that the LORD has set apart for Himself him who is godly; the LORD will hear when I call to Him.

Psalm 4:3 NKJV

Once you were not a people, but now you are God's people; once you had not received mercy, but now you have received mercy.

1 Peter 2:10 ESV

God is faithful, who has called you into fellowship with his Son, Jesus Christ our Lord.

1 Corinthians 1:9 NIV

HE BLESSES EVERY DAY OF OUR LIVES

The curse of the LORD is on the house of the wicked, but He blesses the home of the just.

Proverbs 3:33 NKJV

"Blessed are those who hunger and thirst for righteousness, for they shall be satisfied."

Matthew 5:6 ESV

May you be blessed by the LORD, the Maker of heaven and earth.

Psalm 115:15 NIV

Blessed are those who trust in the LORD and have made the LORD their hope and confidence.

Jeremiah 17:7 NLT

HE BLESSES EVERY DAY OF OUR LIVES

Blessed are those whose way is blameless, who walk in the law of the LORD!

Psalm 119:1 ESV

"God blesses those who are poor and realize their need for Him, for the Kingdom of Heaven is theirs."

Matthew 5:3 NLT

Oh, taste and see that the LORD is good; blessed is the man who trusts in Him!

Psalm 34:8 NKJV

From His abundance we have all received one gracious blessing after another.

John 1:16 NLT

The LORD will indeed give what is good, and our land will yield its harvest.

Psalm 85:12 NIV

All praise to God, the Father of our Lord Jesus Christ, who has blessed us with every spiritual blessing in the heavenly realms because we are united with Christ.

Ephesians 1:3 NLT

When You open Your hand, You satisfy the hunger and thirst of every living thing. The LORD is righteous in everything He does; He is filled with kindness.

Psalm 145:16-17 NLT

HE BLESSES EVERY DAY OF OUR LIVES

The blessing of the LORD brings wealth, without painful toil for it.

Proverbs 10:22 NIV

The LORD bless you and keep you; the LORD make His face shine upon you, and be gracious to you; the LORD lift up His countenance upon you, and give you peace.

Numbers 6:24-26 NKJV

The LORD is my chosen portion and my cup; You hold my lot. The lines have fallen for me in pleasant places; indeed, I have a beautiful inheritance.

Psalm 16:5-6 ESV

"Blessed are the meek, for they will inherit the earth."

Matthew 5:5 NIV

"Blessed are the pure in heart, for they shall see God."

Matthew 5:8 NKJV

"God blesses those who are merciful, for they will be shown mercy."

Matthew 5:7 NLT

"Blessed are those who mourn, for they shall be comforted."

Matthew 5:4 ESV

Surely *goodness* and
mercy shall follow me
all the days of my life;
and I will dwell in the
house of the LORD *forever.*

PSALM 23:6

Give thanks to the Lord, for He is good; His love endures forever.

Psalm 107:1 NIV

The LORD is good to everyone. He showers compassion on all His creation. All of Your works will thank You, LORD, and Your faithful followers will praise You.

Psalm 145:9-10 NLT

Just then a man came up to Jesus and asked, "Teacher, what good thing must I do to get eternal life?" "Why do you ask Me about what is good?" Jesus replied. "There is only One who is good. If you want to enter life, keep the commandments."

Matthew 19:16-17 NIV

GOD IS GOOD

Truly God is good to Israel, to such as are pure in heart.

Psalm 73:1 NKJV

His divine power has given us everything we need for a godly life through our knowledge of Him who called us by His own glory and goodness.

2 Peter 1:3 NIV

For the LORD God is a sun and shield; the LORD bestows favor and honor; no good thing does He withhold from those whose walk is blameless.

Psalm 84:11 NIV

GOD IS GOOD

You are good, and what You do is good; teach me Your decrees.

Psalm 119:68 NIV

Gladden the soul of Your servant, for to You, O Lord, do I lift up my soul. For You, O Lord, are good and forgiving, abounding in steadfast love to all who call upon You.

Psalm 86:4-5 ESV

Good and upright is the LORD; therefore He instructs sinners in His ways. He guides the humble in what is right and teaches them His way.

Psalm 25:8-9 NIV

Every good gift and every perfect gift is from above, and comes down from the Father of lights, with whom there is no variation or shadow of turning.

James 1:17 NKJV

The LORD is good, a strong refuge when trouble comes. He is close to those who trust in Him.

Nahum 1:7 NLT

The LORD said, "I will cause all My goodness to pass in front of you, and I will proclaim My name, the LORD, in your presence. I will have mercy on whom I will have mercy, and I will have compassion on whom I will have compassion."

Exodus 33:19 NIV

GOD IS GOOD

Oh, how abundant is Your goodness, which You have stored up for those who fear You and worked for those who take refuge in You, in the sight of the children of mankind! In the cover of Your presence You hide them from the plots of men; You store them in Your shelter from the strife of tongues.

Psalm 31:19-20 ESV

"Why do you call Me good?" Jesus asked. "Only God is truly good."

Mark 10:18 NLT

The LORD is good; His mercy is everlasting, and His truth endures to all generations.

Psalm 100:5 NKJV

GOD IS MERCIFUL

God saved us and called us to live a holy life. He did this, not because we deserved it, but because that was His plan from before the beginning of time – to show us His grace through Christ Jesus.

2 Timothy 1:9 NLT

"My grace is sufficient for you, for My power is made perfect in weakness."

2 Corinthians 12:9 NIV

"The LORD! The God of compassion and mercy! I am slow to anger and filled with unfailing love and faithfulness."

Exodus 34:6 NLT

GOD IS MERCIFUL

Because of His great love for us, God, who is rich in mercy, made us alive with Christ even when we were dead in transgressions – it is by grace you have been saved.

Ephesians 2:4-5 NIV

Let us then with confidence draw near to the throne of grace, that we may receive mercy and find grace to help in time of need.

Hebrews 4:16 ESV

The LORD longs to be gracious to you; therefore He will rise up to show you compassion. For the LORD is a God of justice. Blessed are all who wait for Him!

Isaiah 30:18 NIV

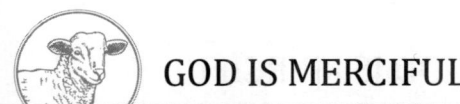
Let the wicked forsake their ways and the unrighteous their thoughts. Let them turn to the LORD, and He will have mercy on them, and to our God, for He will freely pardon.

Isaiah 55:7 NIV

To each one of us grace was given according to the measure of Christ's gift.

Ephesians 4:7 NKJV

Know that the LORD your God, He is God, the faithful God who keeps covenant and mercy for a thousand generations with those who love Him and keep His commandments.

Deuteronomy 7:9 NKJV

GOD IS MERCIFUL

God is able to make all grace abound to you, so that having all sufficiency in all things at all times, you may abound in every good work.

2 Corinthians 9:8 ESV

The LORD takes pleasure in those who fear Him, in those who hope in His mercy. Praise the LORD, O Jerusalem! Praise your God, O Zion!

Psalm 147:11-12 NKJV

When the kindness and love of God our Savior appeared, He saved us, not because of righteous things we had done, but because of His mercy.

Titus 3:4-5 NIV

GOD IS MERCIFUL

The steadfast love of the LORD never ceases; His mercies never come to an end; they are new every morning; great is Your faithfulness. "The LORD is my portion," says my soul, "therefore I will hope in Him."

Lamentations 3:22-24 ESV

All praise to God, the Father of our Lord Jesus Christ. It is by His great mercy that we have been born again, because God raised Jesus Christ from the dead.

1 Peter 1:3 NLT

I have trusted in Your mercy; my heart shall rejoice in Your salvation.

Psalm 13:5 NKJV

A PLACE IN THE HOUSE OF THE LORD

For we know that if the tent that is our earthly home is destroyed, we have a building from God, a house not made with hands, eternal in the heavens.

2 Corinthians 5:1 ESV

I heard a loud voice from the throne saying, "Look! God's dwelling place is now among the people, and He will dwell with them. They will be His people, and God Himself will be with them and be their God."

Revelation 21:3 NIV

No eye has seen, no ear has heard, and no mind has imagined what God has prepared for those who love Him.

1 Corinthians 2:9 NLT

A PLACE IN THE HOUSE OF THE LORD

"Then the King will say to those on His right hand, 'Come, you blessed of My Father, inherit the kingdom prepared for you from the foundation of the world: for I was hungry and you gave Me food; I was thirsty and you gave Me drink; I was a stranger and you took Me in; I was naked and you clothed Me; I was sick and you visited Me; I was in prison and you came to Me.'"

Matthew 25:34-36 NKJV

Jesus answered him, "Truly I tell you, today you will be with Me in Paradise."

Luke 23:43 NIV

"Blessed are you who are poor, for yours is the kingdom of God."

Luke 6:20 NIV

A PLACE IN THE HOUSE OF THE LORD

"People will come from all over the world – from east and west, north and south – to take their places in the Kingdom of God. And note this: Some who seem least important now will be the greatest then, and some who are the greatest now will be least important then."

Luke 13:29-30 NLT

"In My Father's house are many mansions; if it were not so, I would have told you. I go to prepare a place for you. And if I go and prepare a place for you, I will come again and receive you to Myself; that where I am, there you may be also. And where I go you know, and the way you know."

John 14:2-4 NKJV

A PLACE IN THE HOUSE OF THE LORD

For our citizenship is in heaven, from which we also eagerly wait for the Savior, the Lord Jesus Christ, who will transform our lowly body that it may be conformed to His glorious body, according to the working by which He is able even to subdue all things to Himself.

Philippians 3:20-21 NKJV

We have a priceless inheritance – an inheritance that is kept in heaven for you, pure and undefiled, beyond the reach of change and decay. And through your faith, God is protecting you by His power until you receive this salvation, which is ready to be revealed on the last day for all to see. So be truly glad. There is wonderful joy ahead, even though you must endure many trials for a little while.

1 Peter 1:4-6 NLT

A PLACE IN THE HOUSE OF THE LORD

God raised us up with Christ and seated us with Him in the heavenly realms in Christ Jesus, in order that in the coming ages He might show the incomparable riches of His grace, expressed in His kindness to us in Christ Jesus.

Ephesians 2:6-7 NIV

"Let the little children come to Me, and do not forbid them; for of such is the kingdom of God. Assuredly, I say to you, whoever does not receive the kingdom of God as a little child will by no means enter it."

Mark 10:14-15 NKJV

"Not everyone who calls out to Me, 'Lord! Lord!' will enter the Kingdom of Heaven. Only those who actually do the will of My Father in heaven will enter."

Matthew 7:21 NLT

ETERNAL LIFE WITH THE SHEPHERD

"Whoever drinks of this water will thirst again, but whoever drinks of the water that I shall give him will never thirst. But the water that I shall give him will become in him a fountain of water springing up into everlasting life."

John 4:13-14 NKJV

"Everyone who lives in Me and believes in Me will never ever die."

John 11:26 NLT

"Truly, truly, I say to you, whoever hears My word and believes Him who sent Me has eternal life. He does not come into judgment, but has passed from death to life."

John 5:24 ESV

ETERNAL LIFE WITH THE SHEPHERD

The wages of sin is death, but the free gift of God is eternal life through Christ Jesus our Lord.

Romans 6:23 NLT

"For God so loved the world that He gave His one and only Son, that whoever believes in Him shall not perish but have eternal life."

John 3:16 NIV

"Indeed, the time is coming when all the dead in their graves will hear the voice of God's Son, and they will rise again. Those who have done good will rise to experience eternal life, and those who have continued in evil will rise to experience judgment."

John 5:28-29 NLT

ETERNAL LIFE WITH THE SHEPHERD

"I give them eternal life, and they shall never perish; no one will snatch them out of My hand. My Father, who has given them to Me, is greater than all; no one can snatch them out of My Father's hand. I and the Father are one."

John 10:28-30 NIV

He who believes in the Son has everlasting life; and he who does not believe the Son shall not see life, but the wrath of God abides on him.

John 3:36 NKJV

I write these things to you who believe in the name of the Son of God so that you may know that you have eternal life.

1 John 5:13 NIV